How Quick is Quick?

Science Projects with Time

ROBERT GARDNER

ILLUSTRATED BY TOM LABAFF

Enslow Elementary

an imprint of

 Enslow Publishers, Inc.

40 Industrial Road
Box 398
Berkeley Heights, NJ 07922
USA

Enslow Elementary, an imprint of Enslow Publishers, Inc.

Enslow Elementary® is a registered trademark of Enslow Publishers, Inc.

Library of Congress Cataloging-in-Publication Data

Gardner, Robert, 1929– author.
  [It's about time science projects]
  How quick is quick? : science projects with time / Robert Gardner.
    pages cm. — (Hot science experiments)
  "Originally published as It's about time science projects: How Long Does It Take? in 2003."
  Summary: "Simple science experiments about measurement of time using everyday items with many experiments that can be turned into science fair projects."— Provided by publisher.
  Audience: K to grade 3
  Includes bibliographical references and index.
  ISBN 978-0-7660-6610-6
  1. Time measurements—Experiments—Juvenile literature. 2. Clocks and watches—Experiments—Juvenile literature. 3. Science projects—Juvenile literature. I. Title.
  QB209.5.G37 2015
  529.7'078—dc23
                    2014026880

Future editions:
Paperback ISBN: 978-0-7660-6611-3
EPUB ISBN: 978-0-7660-6612-0
Single-User PDF ISBN: 978-0-7660-6613-7
Multi-User PDF ISBN: 978-0-7660-6614-4

Printed in the United States of America
102014 Bang Printing, Brainerd, Minn.
10 9 8 7 6 5 4 3 2 1

Illustration Credits: Tom Labaff (tomlabaff.com)

Cover Credits: Tom Labaff (tomlabaff.com)

Contents

Contains ideas for science fair projects.

Introduction

Time sometimes goes so slowly we say it drags. Sometimes it flies by. What do you think time is? Although we live by it and talk about it, time is hard to describe. But even if we cannot say what it is, we can measure time. We mark the passing of time in seconds, minutes, hours, days, weeks, and years.

Before people had electric clocks and watches, they kept track of time in many ways. They watched the sun move across the sky. They watched the seasons change. Some found they could use water or sand to measure time's passing.

In this book you will learn about time by doing experiments. You will build some very simple clocks, clocks that have no hands. You will try to guess (estimate) the passing of time. You will learn how to measure the times it takes to blink, react to a signal, breathe, and run different distances.

Entering a Science Fair

Some of the experiments in this book might give you ideas for a science fair project. Those experiments are marked with a 🎗 symbol. Remember, judges at science fairs like experiments that are imaginative. It is hard to be creative if you are not interested in your project. So pick a subject that you enjoy and want to know more about.

You can add to the value of your experiment by keeping notes. Set up an experiment notebook and record your work carefully. As you do some of these experiments, you will think of new questions that you can answer with experiments of your own. Go ahead and do these experiments (with your parents' or teacher's permission). You are starting to have the kind of curiosity that is shared by all scientists.

If you enter a science fair, you should read some of the books listed in the back of this book. They will give you helpful hints and lots of useful information about science fairs. You will learn how to prepare appealing reports that include charts and graphs. You will also learn how to set up and display your work, how to present your project, and how to talk with judges and visitors.

Safety First

As you do the activities and experiments in this or any other book, do them safely. Remember the rules listed below and follow them closely.

1. Any experiments that you do should be done under the supervision of a parent, teacher, or another adult.

2. Read all instructions carefully. If you have questions, check with an adult. Do not take chances.

3. If you work with a friend who enjoys science too, keep a serious attitude while experimenting. Fooling around can be dangerous to you and to others.

4. Keep the area where you are experimenting clean and organized. When you have finished, clean up and put away the materials you were using.

Time Before Clocks

When you hear the word "time," you probably think of a clock or a watch. But even very simple mechanical clocks did not exist until about six hundred years ago. Humans first measured time in days or months. A day was the time between one sunrise and the next. The time between one full moon and the next was a month. The moon's cycle, from one full moon to the next, is twenty-nine and a half days. How do you think early humans could tell when a year had passed?

The first devices that might be considered clocks are sundials. You can make a simple sun "clock."

Let's Get Started!

1. Place a large sheet of cardboard on a sunny, level lawn or terrace. Put stones on the corners of the cardboard so it will not blow away.

2. Push the tip of an upright pencil through the center of the cardboard. As you can see, the pencil casts a shadow on the cardboard. What happens to the shadow as time passes and the sun moves across the sky?

In the next experiment you will use the pencil's shadow to measure time.

> **WHAT YOU NEED:**
>
> - large sheet of cardboard
>
> - sunny, level lawn or terrace
>
> - stones to hold down the cardboard
>
> - pencil

Measuring Time with the Sun

Start this experiment early, at 6, 7, or 8 A.M.

Let's Get Started!

1. To make a sun clock, tape a large sheet of wrapping paper over the cardboard from the first experiment.

2. Push the pencil through the center of the paper and cardboard.

3. Place the cardboard on sunny, level ground. Use another pencil to outline the upright pencil's shadow. Write the time next to the shadow. Do this each hour throughout the day. By day's end, you will have a clock like the one in the drawing.

WHAT YOU NEED:

- large sheet of wrapping paper
- cardboard from first experiment
- 2 pencils
- sunny, level ground
- clock or watch
- plastic sheet
- stones to hold down the plastic sheet

4. Look at the clock you have made. When is the clock's "hand" (the shadows you marked) shortest? Longest? Can you see the pattern the sun makes as it moves across the sky?

5. Do not move the cardboard. Cover it with a plastic sheet. Put stones at the corners of the sheet to protect the paper from dampness. On the next sunny day, remove the plastic and watch the sun clock during the day. Can it be used to tell time?

6. Cover the sun clock again. After a few days, remove the plastic and watch the sun clock. Can it still be used to tell time? What has happened?

sun clock

sun dial

Ideas for Your Science Fair

Early humans had no watches. How do you think they divided a day into hours on their sun clocks?

Examine a sundial. How does it differ from your sun clock? Does it keep time better than your sun clock?

A Water Clock

Sun clocks and sundials did not work at night or on cloudy days. People needed a way to measure time when the sun was not out. Water clocks met that need. They were invented about thirty-five hundred years ago. You can make a simple water clock.

Let's Get Started!

1. Use the smallest nail you can find to make a hole in the bottom of a Styrofoam cup. Push the tip of the nail through the bottom of the cup from the inside to the outside.

2. Put a piece of masking tape straight up the side of a tall clear jar.

3. Starting from the bottom of the jar, make lines on the tape one centimeter (a half inch) apart.

4. Put your finger over the hole in the cup and fill it with water. Support the cup on two small sticks or toothpicks across the mouth of the jar, as shown in the drawing.

5. Using a clock or watch that can measure time in seconds, record the time it takes for the water level in the jar to reach the first line. Then record how long it takes the water level to reach the second line, the third line, and so on. How does the time for the water to reach the first line compare with the time to reach the second, third, fourth, and other lines? Are the times different? Can you explain why the times might be different?

toothpicks

A Problem with Water Clocks

WHAT YOU NEED:
- an ADULT
- a partner
- small nail
- coffee can
- pliers
- sponge
- water
- sink
- ruler
- stopwatch or watch that can measure seconds

The simple water clock you built in the last experiment did not keep good time. It took longer for water to reach the second line than the first. You can do another experiment to find out why.

Let's Get Started!

1. **Ask an adult** to use a small nail to make a hole in the bottom of a coffee can. Pliers can be used to push the nail through the can from the inside to the outside.

2. The hole's edge is sharp, so press a sponge under the hole and fill the can with water.

3. While holding the can over a sink, ask a partner to measure the height of the water in the can with a ruler.

4. Remove the sponge and time how long it takes for the can to empty.

5. Add water to the can until the water is half as high as it was before. Repeat the experiment, timing how long it takes to empty the can. Does cutting in half the height of the water cut in half the time it takes for the can to empty?

6. Repeat the experiment once more with the water one quarter as deep as it was the first time. How long does it take for the can to empty? How does this time compare with the time when the can held four times as much water? Does the height of the water affect the water clock's measurement of time?

full   ½ full   ¼ full

Idea for Your Science Fair
Can you make a better water clock?

A Sand Clock

WHAT YOU NEED:

- hourglass
- stopwatch or watch that can measure seconds
- very dry sand or salt
- clean, dry baby food jar
- scissors
- heavy paper
- hole punch
- masking tape

The hourglass was invented more than thirty-five hundred years ago. These sand "clocks" are still used today. You may have a small one to measure the time it takes to play a game. If you have one, use a stopwatch to find out how long it takes all of the sand to flow through the narrow opening to the bottom half.

Let's Get Started!

1. To make a sand clock, pour very dry sand or salt into a clean, dry baby food jar.

2. Using scissors, cut a piece of heavy paper that will cover the mouth of the jar.

3. Make a hole in the center of the paper with a hole punch. Cover the mouth of the jar with the paper.

4. Set an identical jar on top of the first one that holds the sand or salt.

5. Use masking tape to tape the mouths of the jars firmly together.

6. Turn the jars over and watch the sand fall into the lower jar. How much time does your sand clock measure? Turn your sand clock over again. Does it always measure the same time? How can you change it to measure a different amount of time?

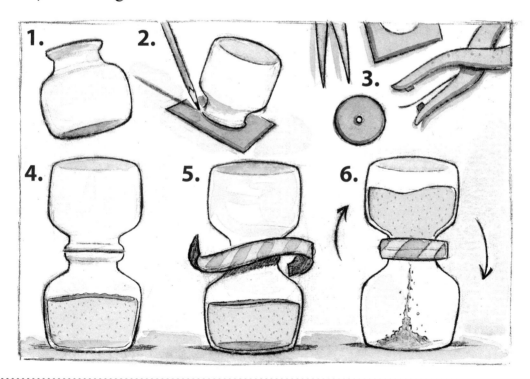

Idea for Your Science Fair

How would you build an hourglass—a sand clock that measures one hour?

A Candle Clock

Oil lamps and candles were once used to measure time. As an oil-lamp "clock" burned, the level of the oil in its glass tank fell. Time was measured by the change in the oil level. How fast the oil burned depended on the amount of wick exposed to the air. Therefore, the wick had to be carefully adjusted before it was lit.

Candles, too, can be used to measure time. A candle will burn quite steadily in a room without drafts. The decreasing height of a candle can be used to measure time.

WHAT YOU NEED:
- an ADULT
- matches
- candle
- ruler
- clock or watch
- pin

Let's Get Started!

1. To make a candle "clock," measure the height of a candle. Measure from the top of the candle holder to the top of the candle, as shown in the drawing.

2. **Ask an adult** to light the candle. Let it burn for exactly one hour. **Do not leave the burning candle unattended.**

3. Remeasure the candle. What length of candle burned away in one hour?

4. Using a ruler and a pin, make marks on the candle to predict how short the candle will be after burning for one, two, and three hours. Light the candle and test your predictions. Were they accurate?

oil lamp

height

Idea for Your Science Fair

In the last few experiments, you made several ancient timekeeping devices. Which would you use to measure hours? Minutes? Which device do you think is the most accurate timekeeper?

Heart Time

You can hear someone else's heartbeat by placing your ear against his chest. Try it. What do you hear?

At one time or another, you have felt your own heart beating. It may have been after running a race or when you were scared. You can feel your heartbeat at other times, too, by taking your pulse. You have probably had a doctor or a nurse take your pulse. But you can feel your own or someone else's pulse very easily.

Let's Get Started!

1. Place your middle and ring fingers on the inside of your own or someone else's wrist. Your fingers should be about an inch behind the thumb side of your palm, as shown in the drawing. Can you feel your pulse? Can you feel someone else's pulse?

2. To convince yourself that a pulse is caused by a heartbeat, listen to a person's heart while feeling his pulse. You will feel the pulse almost immediately after hearing the heartbeat.

3. Use a stopwatch or watch with a second hand to count the number of times your heart beats in one minute. How could you use your heart as a "clock"?

4. Count the number of times other people's hearts beat in one minute. Do their heart clocks agree with yours?

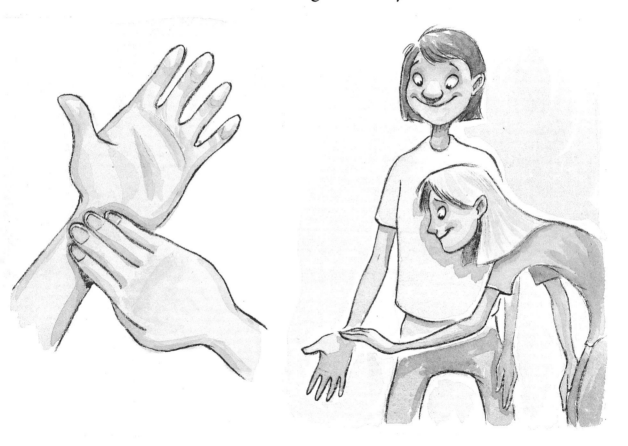

Idea for Your Science Fair
What happens to your heart clock after you exercise?

From Heart Clock to Pendulum Clock

In 1581, an Italian scientist named Galileo sat in church watching a lamp swinging on a chain. Using his pulse, he measured the time it took for the lamp to make one full swing—back and forth. He found that the time was the same whether the lamp moved in a long or a short swing.

You can build a simple pendulum (from the Latin word *pendere,* "to weigh") to see if Galileo was right.

WHAT YOU NEED:

- an ADULT
- long piece of thread
- metal washer
- sharp knife
- tongue depressor
- tape
- refrigerator or high shelf, counter, or table
- meterstick or yardstick
- ruler
- stopwatch or watch that can measure seconds

Let's Get Started!

1. Tie a long piece of thread to a metal washer. The washer will be the pendulum bob.

2. **Ask an adult** to use a sharp knife to make a narrow slit in one end of a tongue depressor. Tape the other end of the tongue depressor to the top of a refrigerator or other high surface.

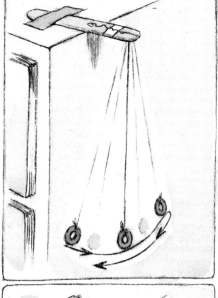

3. Slide the free end of the thread into the slit. The bob should hang about a meter (yard) below the tongue depressor. Tape the free end of the thread to the tongue depressor so the length of the pendulum cannot change.

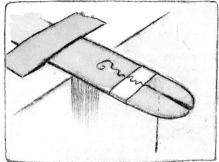

4. Pull the bob back about 2 centimeters (1 inch) and release it. Use a stopwatch or watch that can measure seconds to find the time it takes for the pendulum to make ten complete swings—back and forth. (One swing takes too little time to measure accurately.)

5. Now pull the bob back 10 centimeters (4 inches) and repeat the experiment. Was Galileo correct? Does the distance a pendulum bob swings affect the time it takes to make one complete swing?

A Pendulum Clock

Does the length of a pendulum affect its swing time?

WHAT YOU NEED:

- pendulum from the last experiment
- meterstick or yardstick
- ruler
- stopwatch or watch that can measure seconds

Let's Get Started!

1. Use the pendulum from the last experiment. Adjust the thread until the length of the pendulum is exactly 100 centimeters ($39\frac{3}{8}$ inches). (Measure from the tongue depressor to the center of the washer.)

2. Pull the bob several centimeters to the side and release it. Measure and record the time it takes for the pendulum to make ten complete swings (back and forth). How long does it take this pendulum to make one complete swing? (Divide the time by 10.)

3. Shorten the length of the pendulum to 50 centimeters ($19\frac{11}{16}$ inches). Does this change the time it takes the pendulum to make one complete swing? If it does, is the time longer or shorter?

4. Make the pendulum longer than a meter. Do you think the swing time will be more or less than two seconds? Try it. Were you right?

5. Make a pendulum that has a swing time of exactly one second. Once you succeed, measure your pendulum. How long is it?

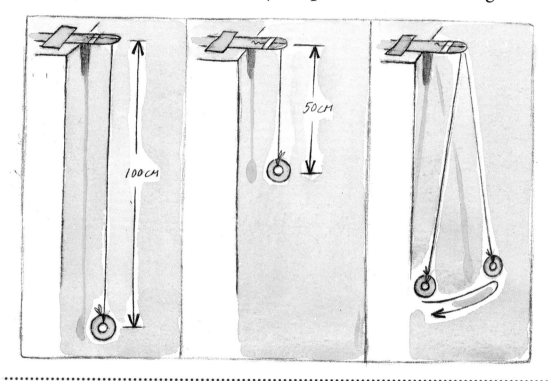

Ideas for Your Science Fair

A grandfather clock is a pendulum clock. What could you do to make such a clock run fast? What could you do to make it run slow?

Does the weight of the bob affect a pendulum's swing time? How can you find out?

Running Time

An Olympic sprinter can run 100 meters in 10 seconds or less. How long does it take you to run 100 meters?

Let's Get Started!

1. If you cannot find a 100-meter track, you can use a football field. The distance from one goal line to the end of the opposite end zone is 110 yards. That is just a bit more than 100 meters. Have a friend with a stopwatch or a watch with a second hand measure the time it takes you to run 100 meters. How long did it take you? How long does it take your friend? How much longer than an Olympic sprinter does it take you to run 100 meters? How about your friend?

2. On a football field, 200 meters is approximately three fourths of the distance around the field, as shown in the

drawing. How long will it take you to run 200 meters? Try it. Were you right? How long does it take your friend?

3. On a football field, 1,000 meters (1 kilometer) is three times around the field plus another 70 yards (see drawing). How long do you think it will take to run 1,000 meters? Will it take ten times as long as it did to run 100 meters? Try it. Were you right? How long does it take your friend?

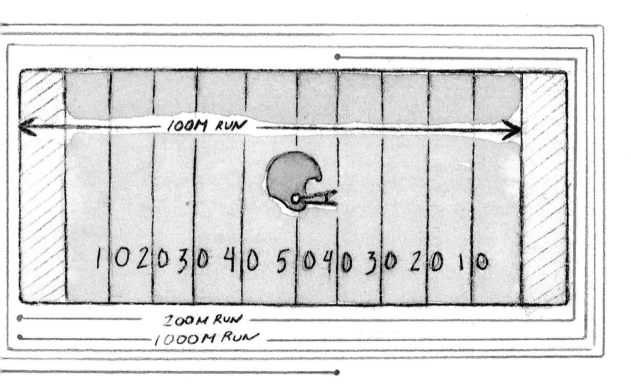

Time to Breathe

Normally, you are not aware of breathing. You inhale (take air into your lungs) and exhale (release air from your lungs) without thinking. It is lucky that breathing is automatic. If we had to concentrate on breathing, we would not have time to do much else.

How long does it take to breathe (inhale and exhale) once?

WHAT YOU NEED:
- a friend
- watch that can measure seconds

Let's Get Started!

1. Ask a friend to lie on a couch or floor and relax. Each time she inhales, you will see her stomach rise. Using a watch, count the number of times your friend inhales and exhales in one minute (60 seconds).

2. How long does it take your friend to breathe (inhale and exhale) once? Divide 60 seconds by the number of times your friend inhaled. For example, if your friend inhaled twelve times in one minute:

60 seconds ÷ 12 = 5 seconds.

How long does it take you to breathe once?

28

3. Ask your friend to exercise for a few minutes, maybe by doing jumping jacks. Immediately after she exercises, ask her to lie down. Count the number of times she breathes in one minute. How does exercising affect the time it takes her to inhale and exhale once? You can figure that out with arithmetic. Does exercise affect breathing in any other way?

4. When your friend is breathing normally again, ask her to stand for five minutes. Then measure her breathing time while she stands. Does she take the same time to breathe when standing as when lying down? Does she take the same time to breathe when sitting as when standing?

stomach rises during inhale

Quick as a Wink or a Squeeze

WHAT YOU NEED:

- a friend
- watch that can measure seconds
- clock with a second hand
- about 20 people

"Quick as a wink!" is a common saying. But how long does it take to wink?

Let's Get Started!

1. Have a friend look at a watch that can measure seconds. When your friend says "Go," wink twenty times as fast as you can. As you wink the twentieth time, say "Stop!" When your friend hears "Stop!" he should note how many seconds have passed since he said "Go."

2. Using the time he measured, you can use arithmetic to figure out how long it takes you to wink once. Divide the total time by 20 to find the time it takes to wink once.

3. Repeat the experiment with your friend doing the winking and you the timing. How does your friend's wink time compare with yours?

4. To measure the time it takes for a person to squeeze someone's hand, have about twenty people stand in a circle holding hands. When the second hand of the clock is at a convenient position, you make the first squeeze with your right hand. The person whose hand you squeezed should use his right hand to squeeze the left hand of the next person. Everyone squeezes a hand in turn. The "squeeze" goes around the circle until it reaches your left hand. When you feel the squeeze, note the time that has passed.

How can you use the time that passed to find the time it takes to squeeze someone's hand?

Time to Fall

Does it take an object twice as long to fall twice as far? To help you find out, you can measure time by counting.

WHAT YOU NEED:

- an ADULT
- clock or watch that can measure seconds
- tennis ball or baseball
- meterstick or yardstick

Let's Get Started!

1. Count "one, two, three, four, five" as fast as you can. You will find it takes about one second to count to five rapidly. To test this way to measure time, look at a clock or watch with a second hand as you count. Count to five as fast as you can ten times. That should take about ten seconds. Since counting to five takes one second, each count is one fifth of a second.

2. Hold a tennis ball or baseball 1 meter (3 feet, 3 inches) above the floor. Release the ball and begin counting right away. Stop counting when the ball hits the floor. Repeat your measurements several times to be sure the time is correct.

3. Ask an adult to drop the ball from a height of 2 meters (6 feet, 6 inches). How long does it take to fall 2 meters? How do your results compare with those in the table to the right? Does the ball take twice as long to fall 2 meters?

Time to fall (using a stopwatch)	
Height (meters)	Time (seconds)
1.0	0.45
2.0	0.64

Idea for Your Science Fair

Do you think a light ball falls faster or slower than a heavier one? Design an experiment to find out.

2 M

1 M

How Fast Can You React?

How long does it take for you to react to a command?

....

Let's Get Started!

1. Ask a friend to hold a smooth yardstick upright a few feet off the ground. He should hold the top of the yardstick. Hold your fingers and thumb on opposite sides of the bottom of the yardstick. Do not touch the stick.

2. Close your eyes. Your friend will say "Go!" at the moment he releases the yardstick. When you hear "Go!"

WHAT YOU NEED:
- a friend
- smooth yardstick

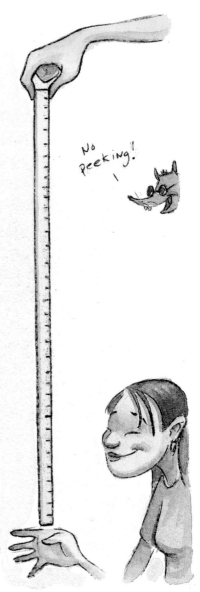

react by closing your thumb and fingers to catch the falling yardstick.

3. Open your eyes and look at the point where you caught the yardstick. Using the chart on the next page, you can find your reaction time.

4. Switch places with your friend. What is your friend's reaction time?

Distance yardstick fell (inches)	Reaction time (seconds)
6	.018 (18/100)
9	0.22 (22/100)
12	0.25 (25/100)
15	0.28 (28/100)
18	0.31 (31/100)
21	0.33 (33/100)
24	0.35 (35/100)

Ideas for Your Science Fair

Test a number of people. Do girls react faster than boys? Do adults react faster than children?

Do you think a person can react quickly enough to catch a dollar bill before it falls through her hand?

Decay Time

Rotten apples and moldy bread are foods that are decaying. How long does it take things to decay?

Let's Get Started!

1. Gather a slice of bread, a slice of apple, a lettuce leaf, pieces of cotton and nylon cloth, a small magazine, and a plastic bag.

2. Put each item on an aluminum pie pan. Cover with another pie pan.

3. Put all the pans in a warm place where you can look at them often. Be sure pets and young children cannot reach the pans.

4. Do any items appear to be decaying after one day? Which are clearly decaying after a week? After a month? Which items show no evidence of decay after two or more months?

WHAT YOU NEED:
- slice of bread
- slice of apple
- lettuce leaf
- pieces of cotton and nylon cloth
- small magazine
- plastic bag
- aluminum pie pans
- plastic containers
- water
- refrigerator
- woods or other place with fallen leaves
- garden gloves

5. Find a piece of bread to which no ingredient to prevent mold has been added (an adult can help you check the label for preservatives).

6. Leave the bread in an open place for several hours. Then break the bread in half.

7. Put each half in a plastic container, add a few drops of water, cover, and seal.

8. Put one container in a refrigerator. Put the other in a warm place. Does temperature affect mold growth?

9. While your experiments are underway, take a walk through some woods. Can you find decaying wood? Put on some garden gloves and pull away upper layers of leaves that have fallen to the ground. Can you find decaying leaves under the more recent ones?

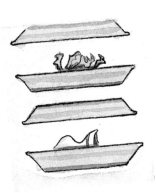

Can you guess what things in a landfill might remain unchanged after many years?

Estimating Time

There is an atomic clock that can measure time to within one second for every million years. We do not need such clocks for most purposes. Some people claim they do not need clocks at all. They say they can estimate (guess) time so well that they never miss an appointment. How well can you estimate time?

WHAT YOU NEED:
- a friend
- watch that can measure seconds
- pen or pencil
- paper

Let's Get Started!

1. Ask a friend with a watch that has a second hand to say "Go!" Do not count seconds or look at a watch. Tell your friend when you think ten seconds have passed. Have her record the actual amount of time that has passed.

2. Continue the experiment by telling your friend when you think a minute has passed and when you think ten minutes have passed. Your friend will record the actual times that have passed. How close were your estimated times to the actual times?

3. It takes about one second to say "twenty-one." If you count seconds this way, are you better able to estimate time?

4. Try estimating the time it takes to do simple tasks such as brushing your teeth, taking a shower, or eating breakfast. Then use a watch to measure the actual times it takes to do these things. How closely do your estimated times agree with the actual times?

Idea for Your Science Fair

Try these same experiments on a number of different people. Are some people better at estimating time than others?

Using Time to Stop Motion

Let's Get Started!

1. **Ask an adult to help you with this experiment.** Find a small electric fan. Be sure the fan blades are covered by a protective screen.

2. Turn on the fan. It probably spins so fast you cannot see the blades. Turn off the fan.

3. Turn on a television in a dark room. Put the fan in front of the television screen.

4. Turn on the fan. Now can you see the fan blades? Do they appear to be stopped or spinning slowly forward or backward?

5. If the fan's speed is adjustable, change it until the blades appear stopped. What happens if you slowly increase or decrease the fan's speed?

WHAT YOU NEED:

- an ADULT
- small electric fan wi[...] blades covered by a protective screen
- television
- dark room

6. Turn the fan off and watch the blades as their speed decreases. You will see them appear to stop, rotate slowly forward or backward, and stop again. They will rotate slowly again, and so on until the fan stops.

Unlike a lightbulb, a television screen does not emit light all the time. Like a strobe light, it emits light many times each second. It happens so fast we do not notice it.

Suppose the light comes on sixty times every second. If the fan is rotating sixty times every second, the fan blades will always appear to be at the same place. What will you see if the fan is turning more than sixty times per second? Less than sixty times per second?

A Year of Change

A day is a measure of time. Early humans called the time from one sunrise to the next a day. The time of sunrise changes. You can do an experiment to find out if the sun's position changes.

WHAT YOU NEED:
- piece of cardboard, about 12 x 8 inches
- nail
- tape
- south–facing window
- sheet of paper
- counter or table
- accurate clock
- paper
- marking pen

Let's Get Started!

1. Take a large piece of cardboard, about 12 x 8 inches. Use a nail to make a hole about 4 inches above the bottom edge of the cardboard.

2. Tape the cardboard to the lower corner of a south-facing window.

3. Tape a sheet of paper to a counter or table under the cardboard on the window.

4. Sunlight coming through the hole will make a bright spot on the paper. At exactly noon, mark the center of the bright spot on the paper with a pen. Write the date by the mark. Do this at noon on every sunny day. (Remember during

Daylight Savings Time to make the mark at 1:00 P.M.) It is all right to skip a few days, but be sure to mark the sun at exactly noon (or 1:00 P.M. during Daylight Savings Time) at least weekly. Always record the date next to the mark. How does the sun's position change? Why do you think it changes?

Idea for Your Science Fair

Continue the experiment for a year. You will find that a figure-eight pattern emerges. Can you find a similar pattern on a globe? Does the pattern on the paper and the globe tell you something about the earth?

Words to Know

atomic clock—A very accurate device that uses radiation released by atoms to measure time.

candle clock—A timepiece in which the passage of time is measured by the change in the length of a candle.

decay—The breakdown of matter, usually through the action of bacteria or fungi.

exhale—To release air from the lungs.

Galileo—An Italian astronomer, physicist, and mathematician who lived from 1564 to 1642. His full name was Galileo Galilei.

globe—A ball-shaped device used to represent the earth.

hourglass—A timepiece in which it takes sand one hour to pass from the upper to the lower part of a container through a narrow opening.

inhale—To take air into the lungs.

oil-lamp clock—A timepiece in which the passage of time is measured by the volume of oil used by the lamp, which burns oil by means of a lighted wick.

pendulum—A weight (called a bob) suspended by a thread, string, or other means so that it can swing freely back and forth.

pendulum clock—A timepiece that uses a pendulum to measure the passage of time.

pulse—An expansion of an artery that can be felt, usually on the lower wrist. The expansion is caused by blood forced into the arteries each time the heart beats.

sand clock—A timepiece in which sand passes from the upper to the lower part of a container through a narrow opening. The time for passage is determined by the amount of sand and the size of the opening.

strobe light—A device that gives off light broken into parts.

sundial—A device that uses the sun to cast a shadow. It uses the shadow to measure the time of day.

water clock—A device that uses water to measure the passage of time.

Further Reading

Brunner-Jass, Renata. *Field of Play: Measuring Distance, Rate, and Time*. Chicago, Ill.: Norwood House Press, 2003.

Graham, John. *Forces and Motion*. London, England: Kingfisher Books Ltd, 2001.

Markle, Sandra. *Measuring Up: Experiments, Puzzles, and Games Exploring Measurement*. New York: Atheneum Books for Young Readers, 1995.

Smoothey, Marion. *Estimating*. New York: Marshall Cavendish, 1994.

VanCleave, Janice. *Janice VanCleave's Guide to the Best Science Fair Projects*. New York: John Wiley & Sons, 1996.

Welch, Catherine. *Forces and Motion: A Question and Answer Book*. North Mankato, Minn.: Capstone Press, 2007.

Quick as Lightning

Thunder is heard shortly after lightning because the air around the lightning bolt is heated to temperatures as high as 54,000°F. The heated air expands suddenly, creating a sound wave.

Since light travels at 186,000 miles per second, you see lightning almost the instant it occurs. But sound travels much more slowly, about 340 m (1,100 feet) per second, which is about one mile in five seconds. If you see lightning, start counting, "One thousand one, one thousand two, one thousand three, . . ." until you hear the thunder. How can you use this technique to estimate the distance to a thunderstorm?

Do not go outside even if a thunderstorm seems far away. Estimate the distance to the storm from inside your house, where it is safer.

Index